GHOST STORIES
OF
LANCASTER, PA

Ghost Stories
of
Lancaster, PA

by Tim Reeser

Ghosts of Lancaster, PA

A candlelight <u>walking tour</u> where stories of haunted houses, eerie cemeteries and lost souls are woven into the history and mystery of one of America's oldest cities.

Tours are available from May - October
717-687-6687
www.ghosttour.com

GHOST STORIES OF LANCASTER, PA

1stSight Press
Box 42 Monocacy, PA 19542

First Printing 2003
Printed in the United States of America
ISBN: 0-9729265-1-8

*To Shirley and Al, for creating
a little corner of heaven in
Hell's Hole*

Front Cover Picture

SOLDIER AND SAILORS MONUMENT
Penn Square, Lancaster City
"Erected in 1874 to honor...Union soldiers of the Civil War...constructed in the Gothic style, and depicts men on pedestals from four branches of the Armed Services: Infantry, Artillery, Cavalry and Navy. Overlooking all stands the genius of Liberty, her sword pointing downward signifying the end of the bitter conflict."

-Monument plaque

Ghost Stories of Lancaster, PA

Contents

1	Legacy of a Haunted City	1
2	The General Returns	8
3	Barton's Banishment	20
4	Old King Cole'	30
5	Cursed	40
6	Bloody End	50
7	Phantoms in the Opera House	62
8	Tales of Strasburg	74
9	Strasburg Cemetery	78
10	Hell's Tunnel	90
11	Mrs. Yates	98
12	Old Jake	112
13	John Funck House	122

HALLOWEEN GREETINGS

1909 postcard from Deutschland

GHOST STORIES OF LANCASTER, PA

Today the name Lancaster conjures images of the Amish, the plain folk of Pennsylvania who have farmed and lived in the area for hundreds of years, changing very little from generation to generation. A huge tourist business has blossomed around their quaint ways and lifestyle, but in searching for ghost stories, we have found there is more to Lancaster.

Small country towns and villages dot the countryside, and the City of Lancaster anchors a strong and robust community that has existed since the earliest days of European exploration and settlement on this continent.

Many of America's most famous names have walked the historic streets of Lancaster...Benjamin Franklin, George Washington, John Hancock, Marquis de Lafayette, Meriweather Lewis, Abraham Lincoln and many more. The old brick colonial buildings that line Lancaster's streets and alleys are filled with stories of intrigue and providence, victory and prosperity, love, and of course, loss...elements that make for great storytelling and most of all... great *ghost stories*.

Has anyone seen George Ross?

Legacy of a Haunted City

Lancaster is one of America's oldest cities. When the Europeans first arrived, Native American settlements covered the area, and a major Indian trail existed where present-day Orange Street runs through the center of the city. In the early 18th century, Lancaster served as the American frontier - the outer edge of civilization. Populated by the Conestoga Indian tribes and rugged pioneers who thrived in the fertile valleys and bountiful forests, the area developed quickly into an important early American outpost.

But this is not a history book. The stories collected here are based on actual paranormal sightings and activity reported around the city of Lancaster. Of course, history lends a certain "credibility" to the supernatural activity, and provides clues to the possible sources of the apparitions, ghosts, phantoms, poltergeists or spirits reported roaming the streets and haunting the buildings of this old city. So, while these stories are steeped in mystery, perhaps poking around the edges of the documented past will shed some light on the hauntings that fascinate those interested in the *other* side of history.

OLD CENTER SQUARE
(PENN SQUARE)

INDIAN WIGWAMS, A HICKORY TREE, AND A SPRING — THAT WAS OLD CENTER SQUARE OR "HICKORY TOWN" PRIOR TO 1730. IN THAT YEAR, HOWEVER, SIGNIFICANT CHANGES OCCURRED AS ANDREW AND JAMES HAMILTON LAID OUT LANCASTER TOWNSTEAD WITH AN OPEN SQUARE, STREETS CROSSING AT RIGHT ANGLES, AND THREE PLOTS DESIGNATED FOR A COURTHOUSE, A JAIL, AND A MARKET AREA. IN 1744, SEVERAL HUNDRED INDIANS FROM THE SIX MOST POWERFUL, CONFEDERATED TRIBES OF THE MIDDLE ATLANTIC INDIANS SIGNED THE TREATY OF SIX NATIONS WITH COLONIAL REPRESENTATIVES FROM PENNSYLVANIA, MARYLAND, AND VIRGINIA. FOLLOWING MEETINGS IN THE OLD COURTHOUSE IN THE SQUARE, THE INDIANS, IN EXCHANGE FOR £1,200, BLANKETS, GUNS, RUM, AND GOLD, RESCINDED THEIR RIGHTS TO DISPUTED LAND IN VIRGINIA AND MARYLAND, RENEWED FORMER TREATIES, AND SWORE ALLEGIANCE TO THE BRITISH AGAINST THE FRENCH.

SAM ADAMS, JOHN ADAMS, CHARLES CARROLL, JOHN HANCOCK, AND ROBERT MORRIS WALKED THROUGH THIS VERY LOCATION ON SEPTEMBER 27, 1777, WHEN LANCASTER WAS HOST TO THE CONTINENTAL CONGRESS. OTHER FAMOUS VISITORS HAVE INCLUDED GEORGE WASHINGTON (1791), ANDREW JACKSON (1819), MARQUIS DE LAFAYETTE (1825), WILLIAM HENRY HARRISON (1836), SAM HOUSTON (1848), ZACHARY TAYLOR (1849), ABRAHAM LINCOLN (1861), ULYSSES S. GRANT (1876), WOODROW WILSON (1895), AND JOHN F. KENNEDY (1960).

DURING THE 18TH AND 19TH CENTURIES, CENTER SQUARE ENJOYED A LOCAL COLOR INDICATIVE OF LANCASTER'S TRADE AND PERSONALITIES. THE SQUARE WAS A PUBLIC MARKET UNTIL A MARKET HOUSE WAS BUILT ON THE NORTHWEST CORNER IN 1757. ROBERT FULTON'S FATHER OWNED A TAILOR SHOP AT THE NORTHEAST CORNER WHILE IN THE SOUTHWEST SECTOR JOSEPH SIMON, INDIAN TRADER, OPERATED ONE OF THE LARGEST TRADING STORES IN THE COLONY.

While still ruled by the British, Lancaster played a key role in the French and Indian Wars. During that time, a horrific incident took place in Lancaster. A massacre of defenseless women, children and men, which was so terrible that even to this day, the ghosts of these unfortunate people are said to haunt the streets of the city.

Soon afterwards the American Revolution also left its mark on Lancaster. For one day, the city served as the capital of the fledgling nation, as members of the Continental Congress fled to York, following the fall of Philadelphia to General Howe and British troops. British prisoners of war were housed in Lancaster at that time, and the young and handsome John Andre became smitten with Peggy

Phantom sirens at Central Market?

Shippen, the beautiful granddaughter of one of Lancaster's most prominent families. Their friendship eventually led to Benedict Arnold's infamous betrayal of his country, and some say the figures of John and Peggy can still be seen walking hand in hand through the old streets of Lancaster as they did in that earlier time.

The war of 1812 saw the emergence of perhaps the city's most well known citizen, James Buchanan, who went on to become the fifteenth President of the United States. He volunteered for the army and headed to Maryland to protect the city of Baltimore after the British burned the nation's new capital in Washington D.C. Following the war, Mr. Buchanan fell in love with and became engaged to Ann Coleman, the daughter of the most powerful and wealthiest man in Lancaster. But the daughters of Robert Coleman were cursed, and their ghosts are said to still wander the streets of the city, pining for their lost lovers.

The Civil War also brought heartbreak and tragedy to Lancaster, as one of the Union Army's most accomplished officers, General John Reynolds, fell to a sniper's bullet on the first day of battle at Gettysburg. Reynolds left behind a secret, which remained unknown until his funeral...a secret that could reveal the reason for the sightings in front of his old home on King Street.

Perhaps the most powerful of these stories is based on the poem "The Legend of the Hounds." A classic ghost story, variations of which probably have been told since the Middle Ages. A story with a strong connection to Lancaster...a story best read on a dark moonless night with the wind howling in the trees, preferably outside, around a campfire, with shadows dancing among the trees.

A multitude of other ghostly sightings have occurred throughout the city. Reportedly built on the site of an old church burial ground, the Courthouse may be haunted by those disturbed spirits. Penn's Square, at the center of town, is also the center of several stories including the ghost of George Ross, signer of the Declaration of Independence, and sighted at the Heritage Center. Long dead firemen still respond to the call at the onetime firehouse, which is now Central Market.

Phantom footsteps in the alley between Central Market and the old Grape Inn.

And a colonial era figure is said to haunt the old Groff & Wolf clothing store, previously known as The Grape, a favorite colonial inn of George Washington.

Elsewhere, the spirit of a long-ago Jewish peddler haunts the site of his murder, near Franklin & Marshall College. The statue on Augusta Bitner's grave in the Lancaster Cemetery roams among the other tombstones on certain days of the year, and the library on Duke Street contains stories other than those in its books.

There are many more ghost stories haunting the city than you will find in *this* book. So if you happen to run into long ago deceased Milton Hershey of chocolate fame or Frank Woolworth of 5&10 Cent renown when out and about in Lancaster, it may just be another story waiting to be told!

Who lurks along King Street?

The General Returns

Reports of a man dressed in uniform strolling along King Street have circulated about Lancaster for over a century. The man appears and disappears suddenly, and many believe that the ghostly figure is none other than the Army General who once lived there.

If unrequited love is reason enough for the unexplained sightings of the shadowy figure spotted distraughtly clutching an object to his heart...an object bestowed upon him by the woman he loved... a woman who suffered an equally sad fate...then perhaps the General *has* returned.

The colonial-era building located at 44 West King Street, just off Penn Square, sits snuggly along a busy commercial block of stores and restaurants. Once the home of General John Fulton Reynolds, today it still stands as testament to one of the heroes of the Civil War, a hero whom some say still wanders the streets of Lancaster. A soldier doomed in his heroic campaign to defend his country, and perhaps caught in an age-Old curse, Reynolds may forever wander in the afterlife, doomed in his search for a lost love.

John Reynolds was born in Lancaster in 1820 and chose a life in the United States military. He graduated from West Point Military Academy in 1841 and served in the Mexican-American War, where he earned several promotions and proved himself a superior tactician. His military career took him across the country from east coast to west coast and back again.

But Reynolds is best known as one of the outstanding Union Army officers of the Civil War. President Lincoln thought so highly of Reynolds' leadership skills, that he offered him command of the entire Union Army. Surprisingly, Reynolds turned him down, unwilling to command without complete control, which Lincoln was unwilling to grant.

In the relatively peaceful period prior to the Civil War, John Reynolds continued to serve in the Army with stops in California and West Point, New York where he taught war tactics. In the 1850s, he also

General John Fulton Reynolds

dabbled in the Pennsylvania iron industry, assuming management control of the Colebrook Furnace. Located in the Lancaster countryside, Colebrook Furnace carried the legacy of a curse, fostered by the deeds of a cruel and fanatical ironmaster from several decades earlier.

At the age of 40, John Reynolds remained a bachelor, still "married to the military." But somewhere around that time, John Reynolds found the love of his life.

Catherine Hewitt, or Kate as he called her, at the young age of just 24 years old, won the career soldier's heart. Attractively small and trim, Kate's blond hair, blue eyes, child-like face and delicate demeanor contrasted sharply with the hulking six-feet tall Army officer's solidly built, narrow-waisted figure topped with dark hair and a neatly groomed beard.

In 1861, John and Kate decided to marry, but the Civil War loomed in Reynolds' future. Nevertheless, they became engaged and exchanged rings.

"Djinn": Also known as a "genie," resides in a bottle...or finger ring, from where it can be called forth to serve the desires of its master.
-Arabic Folklore

John gave Kate his ring from West Point. Kate gave John a gold ring with an inscription that read "Dear Kate" and also a medallion to wear around his neck "to keep him safe." They agreed to marry after the war and planned to honeymoon in Europe.

But the couple kept their engagement a secret. In an era where marriage outside one's faith was discouraged, Kate and John expected resistance from their families. Kate grew up in the Catholic faith, and John grew up in a staunchly religious Protestant family...a large family of brothers and sisters with whom he remained very close. John felt uncertain whether his fiancé would be readily accepted into the family because of her religion.

Before they had the chance to make the announcement, duty called. John Reynolds re-joined the Union Army in its battle against the Confederates. He performed admirably, and his fellow officers and the men he commanded held him in the highest of esteem. Reynolds assumed command of the Left Wing of the Army of the Potomac under the newly assigned commanding officer, General George Meade. As the rebels under General Robert E. Lee invaded the North by advancing into Pennsylvania, General Reynolds and his Left Wing corps gave chase.

Reynolds knew his home territory. He planned to intercept Lee's army and make a stand at Gettysburg. Moving his troops as fast as possible to that small country town, just 50 miles from his home in Lancaster, Reynolds unknowingly began a series of events that would lead to one of the most strategically important battles of the Civil War.

Timing became critical. As the first Confederate troops arrived on the scene on July 1, 1863, Reynolds rushed his troops to the high ground just south of the little village. He realized the tactical importance and military advantage of controlling those hills during the upcoming battle.

He fired off a dispatch to Meade: "...*the enemy are advancing in strong force and that I fear they will get to the heights beyond the town before I can. I will fight them inch by inch and if driven back into town, I will barricade the streets and hold them back as long as possible.*"

General Reynolds succeeded in his bold tactical move. The Union Army attained the high ground before the Confederates could. But he paid for his success. As he rode toward the hill, he stopped for a moment and turned in his saddle to check on his troops. Suddenly, Reynolds fell, shot from his horse, a bullet lodged in his brain. The rifle ball entered behind his right ear, and according to reports there were no signs of bleeding. When turned onto his back, he smiled, gasped once and died.

Reynolds' Monument at Gettysburg

General John F. Reynolds fell as one of the first casualties at the Battle of Gettysburg, and the highest-ranking officer to die from either side. But his quick thinking and rapid move to the heights proved one of the most important maneuvers of the battle. The Confederates were eventually stopped, and Reynolds' leadership early in the battle marked him as one of the heroes of the Battle of Gettysburg.

Removed from the battlefield, embalmed and taken to his sister's house in Philadelphia for public viewing, enormous crowds bid goodbye to Reynolds. On the day of the viewing, a mysterious woman arrived asking to see the coffin.

"If you carry the 91st Psalm with you in the army, bullets will not harm you."
- Superstitions of the Pennsylvania Germans

...Though a thousand fall at my side, though ten thousand are dying around me, the evil will not touch me... Psalm 91

There she stood, John's secret finally revealed. Kate had received word of his death, and for the first time, under the most grievous of circumstances, John's family became aware of Kate, his secret fiancée.

During a long night of grieving, Kate remained next to her lover's coffin. Still overcome by grief the next day, Kate chose not to attend John's funeral in Lancaster.

The young Kate never married. She entered a Catholic convent where she became a teaching nun. A friend of John's visited her several years later and reported that Kate remained as grief stricken as ever over the loss of John.

In 1868, Kate left the convent due to illness. Could it have

> "It is a good omen to dream of the dead – it may foretell of a wedding."
>
> - Superstitions of the Pennsylvania Germans

been melancholia, what we call depression today? Whatever the reason, at the age of 32, Catherine Hewitt disappeared, and no one ever heard from Kate again.

Is it possible that John Reynolds returns in search of his beloved Kate...that he returns again and again hoping to find her waiting for him? Does he impatiently pace up and down King Street, clutching that medallion given to him for protection by Kate...a medallion that failed to save him in his last and finest hour as he maneuvered to defend his country? Is John still waiting, hoping to meet up with Kate...so they can live out their existence together...a life they planned so long ago?

Note:

Some have attributed the heartbreaking story of John Reynolds and Kate Hewitt to the "curse of the hounds" - an interesting and intriguing possibility. Legend says that the inhumane and crazed ironmaster of Colebrook Furnace drove his hunting dogs to a fiery death in the portals of the iron furnace after a failed hunting expedition. Legend also says that ever since, a curse strikes misfortune on the masters of the furnace as retribution for the slaughter of the betrayed hounds. Records show that John Reynolds did have a business arrangement with the Colemans to operate the Colebrook Furnace in the years prior to the Civil War. His tragic fate, as well as Kate's, can only be matched by that of the Coleman family, as told in the Old King Cole' chapter.

St. James Cemetery

Barton's Banishment

For as long as anyone can remember, sightings of apparitions moving about Orange Street, walking side by side, usually hand in hand, are common...and why not? If *you* walk along Orange Street, and happen to step through the black iron gates into the St. James Cemetery at the corner of Duke and Orange Streets and stroll along the brick pathways that meander between the tombstones and crypts marking the graves beneath the majestic trees shading the quiet necropolis, you might just expect to see a ghost...particularly after hearing the stories of those buried there.

St. James Cemetery serves as the final resting place for the wealthy and powerful iron-industry pioneer Robert Coleman and much of his immediate family, including his two daughters Ann and Sarah. Ann left Lancaster and committed suicide after her father's misguided meddling in her love life. The same fate befell her sister Sarah several years later, following similar circumstances.

The Coleman family's strong ties to Lancaster, and Ann and Sarah's equally strong attachment to their lovers, provide likely clues to the identity of the specters seen walking arm in arm on Orange Street, only to disappear as the apparitions near the corner of Duke Street.

Some people claim that the sightings are of the heartbroken Ann Coleman, courted again by the spurned James Buchanan.

Others suspect a secret rendezvous between Sarah Coleman and her forbidden lover

St. James Church

William Muhlenberg, who served as Reverend to the St. James Episcopal Church located next to the cemetery.

But alas, there is another possibility, for if any ghosts are lingering about, one must consider the dichotomy of Thomas Barton's position, a man caught in a time of changing loyalties who refused to betray his motherland, and the ultimately sad ending it produced.

One of the early leaders of the St. James Episcopal Church, Thomas Barton served his parishioners while the colonies were still under British control. He lived in Lancaster with his family for nearly 20 years, and he presided over a growing congregation as the city blossomed.

The Anglican Church functioned as an important extension of British rule, but by the Revolutionary War, this connection to the King

> In 1763, during a Christmas service held at St. James by Thomas Barton, the last members of the Conestoga Indian tribe were being massacred in the old Lancaster jail.

proved a liability for those who would not renounce their loyalty to England. As the discontent grew into revolution, Barton maintained his loyalty to the British Crown, and as one of the few Tories in a city bursting with Patriots loyal to the newly declared nation, Barton found himself an outcast.

Barton refused the oath of allegiance, unwilling to betray the head of his church, the King of England. Marked as a traitor to the cause of the Revolution, the authorities closed St. James and banished Barton from Lancaster. He made his way to New York City, British-held territory at the time, still loyal to god and country, but separated from his children, isolated from his longtime congregation and exiled from his longtime home.

His superiors in the church ordered Barton to return to England. He fought the request and sought permission to stay in the colonies, hoping to return to Lancaster to be reunited with his dearly beloved family.

But Barton never made it back. Before the war ended, he died, never to see any of his family again. Unable to return his body to the rebellious city of Lancaster, the British buried Barton in a New York cemetery.

Barton's request to stay near his loved ones.

To his Excellency Sir Henry CLINTON, K.B., Commander in Chief &c &c &c

The Memorial of Thomas BARTON, Missionary to the Episcopal Churches of Lancaster, Caernarvan, and Pequee, in the Province of Pennsylvania,

Sheweth;

That your Memorialist, having had the Honor, by a Memorial of the 12th Instant, of representing his late and present Situation to their Excellencies his Majesty's Commissioners; and having learned from Mr. EDEN that your Excellency permits him to hope for 'a Chaplaincy if that would be better suited to his Interest & Wishes than a Voyage to England.'

Your Memorialist therefore, desirous of remaining as near, as his safety will admit of, to his Children & other tender Connections, 'till the fate of America shall be determined, pray your Excellency's Indulgence to present such Testimonials and papers, as may encourage him to avail himself of your Excellency's Humanity; And to solicit any Appointment that you may be pleased to think adapted to the present Condition or Misfortunes of

Your Excellency's most respectfull

& most obedient Memorialist

Tho. BARTON

At this point, Barton's story takes a weird twist. If you look closely at the row of tombstones just behind St. James Church, you can see Esther Barton's tombstone, and next to hers, one bearing Thomas Barton's name. But neither lies buried under those markers.

Where are the bodies?

Esther's remains were relocated from her original entombment underneath the pavement in front of the church to an unknown location in the graveyard. And Thomas' remains are buried somewhere in New York, the exact whereabouts unknown, lost when moved from the original place of interment.

Is Thomas finally reunited with his loved ones in the afterlife, happy once again as he strolls the streets where he served so faithfully? Or does he return from his unknown gravesite, searching in the shadows of the St. James Cemetery for his misplaced Esther? Perhaps Thomas has several strong reasons to return to the city he called home, a city he helped nurture as it grew - before his callous and sad separation from Lancaster.

So you decide.

Are the ghostly figures seen so frequently strolling along Orange Street the star-crossed lovers Ann Coleman and hometown President James Buchanan?

Or, does her sister Sarah and the forbidden Reverend William Muhlenberg still meet in the shadows of darkness?

Perhaps, Thomas Barton has finally returned after the ruthless separation from his family, reunited again in Lancaster with his loved ones.

Maybe, just maybe, some other mystery awaits us along Orange Street!

Memorial Stone to
The Rev. Thomas Barton
1730 - 1780

British Missionary who Served
for 19 years with Distinction as Third
Rector of St. James Church 1759-1778
True to his ordination vows, he remained loyal
to the Crown during the American Revolution
Political differences between him and the
Patriot members of his congregation caused
the church to be closed in 1776
for the duration of the War
After his resignation as Rector in 1778, he
was given Military Escort to a point within
the British Lines in New York City and
denied right of return to Penna.
Separated from his children, parishioners
and friends, he became incurably ill and died in 1780
He was a faithful Servant of Jesus Christ
and Valiant Soldier who despite
indescribable suffering and hardship
remained steadfast in his convictions
even to the end

Does the statue on Augusta Bitner's grave walk the
Lancaster Cemetery on certain nights of the year?

Old King Cole'

Old legends die hard, and in some cases, as time passes and cultures change, the long forgotten characters in the story may also change, but the message remains the same. In Northern Europe, an ancient legend known as the Wild Hunt took several forms with the huntsman usually described as a demonic figure roaming the countryside with a pack of lost souls or spirits reincarnated as ghostly hounds. In Germany, the devil himself led the howling "hell-hounds," and in England, a number of legendary figures took charge, including King Arthur and Sir Francis Drake.

Pennsylvania has its own legend comparable to the Wild Hunt as told by George Henry Boker in the poem "The Legend of the Hounds." The story originated in the iron-making region of Lancaster County and involves several well-known figures from Lancaster history, including hometown President James Buchanan, the wealthy Coleman family,

renowned   Episcopalian   clergyman   William
Muhlenberg and local Civil War hero John Reynolds.

The poem recounts the slaughter of a pack of hounds
at Colebrook Furnace, an iron-making facility that
existed for almost a century in the Lancaster
countryside. Perpetrated by the ironmaster, whom
history records as a madman with little regard for
human or animal dignity, he led his pack of faithful
dogs to a fiery death in a
fit of spiteful rage. Since
that horrific act, a series
of   tragic   events
spanning   almost   100

> Wild Hunt: ...a pack of
> spectral hounds that runs
> along the ground or just above
> it, hunting for human souls...
> - Cornish folklore

years, has wreaked havoc on the fate of a number of
people, their families and loved ones, all with a close
association to the Colebrook Furnace as the common
denominator.

Can the depraved acts of one demented soul result in
a curse influencing the lives of so many people who
have but a chance connection to that place?

The legend begins with Robert Coleman, the "Iron
King" of colonial America. Coleman arrived in

Philadelphia from Ireland as a young man with very little money in his pocket and very few prospects for improving his lot. However, before he died in 1825, Coleman amassed a fortune in the iron-making industry in Lancaster County, creating an empire that would make his family arguably the wealthiest in the nation for over a century. But along with that

> tommyknockers: ...a spirit that lives and works in mines...
> - American folklore

wealth came a series of tragedies that some say began with the tragic events at the Colebrook Furnace.

Coleman's wealth grew and his industrial empire expanded as he developed iron-making facilities throughout southeastern Pennsylvania. In 1791, Coleman built the Colebrook Furnace, several miles north of Lancaster City, and some claim that the legendary crazed ironmaster can be traced to Sam Jacobs, hired by the driven, no-nonsense iron baron, Robert Coleman, to run the Colebrook Furnace. Jacobs had the reputation as a hard and cruel taskmaster who ruled with fear and discipline.

> Slave Name: Rebecca
> Slave Sex: Female
> Slave Age: About three months old at Registration.
> Slave Date of Birth: "born in August 1799"
> Slave Status: Slave to age 28
> Slave Description: "Negro female child"
> Slave Notes: 1799 Registration notes "daughter of negro Dinah." Actual registration was made by "Samuel Jacobs, Mount Joy Township, Ironmaster, agent for Robert Coleman of Elizabeth Township, Ironmaster." Mother of Henrietta, born on or about March 19, 1818.
> Date of Record: November 27, 1799
>
> -www.afrolumens.org

Pettifoggery between Coleman and Jacobs?

Known as "Squire" Jacobs for his pack of fine hunting dogs, Boker immortalized the wicked ironmaster in his epic poem. Excerpts from "The Legend of the Hounds" tell the story:

Colebrook Furnace in Cornwall stands
Crouched at the foot of the iron lands,
The wondrous hill of iron ore
That pours its wealth through the furnace-door,

...riches from the portals of hell...

Tortured with fire till a molten flood
So that a gazer looking down
Might think, if fancy helped the spell,
He saw a grate in the roof of hell...

...the despicable ironmaster...

Gold and hunting and potent drink,
And loud-tongued girls, that grin and wink
Over the flagon's dripping brim,
These were the things that busied him.
Strong of sinew and dull of mind,
He blustered around like a winter wind.
You could hear his laugh come on before
While his hounds were off a mile or more;

...and his faithful hounds...

Flora, the leader of his pack,
Followed, a shadow in his track;
Followed despite his kicks and blows,
Paused when he paused, rose when he rose.
Nestled beneath his clumsy feet
And sometimes when her drunken lord
Slid stupefied beneath the board,
And stouter comrades jeered his plight
With pointed thumbs and laughter light,
She howled above the Squire's disgrace,
Or, moaning, licked his flaming face.

...one day the dogs would not hunt...

Amid the cowering dogs he dashed,
Rode over some, cursed all, and lashed
Even Flora until her milky side
With trickling crimson welts was dyed.

If my dogs cannot hunt so well
On earth, another hunt in hell

...he drove the pack to the doors of the furnace...

Into the flames with howl and yell,
Hurled by the rugged firemen, fell
That pack of forty. Better hounds,
Fuller of music, of the sounds,

...until only Flora remained...

"In with her! She's the last and worst:
Mere justice should have sent her first!"
Towards her approached the lathful gang;
But Flora bared her ivory fang,
And snarled a warning. Every hair
That bristled on her said - "Beware!"
She fairly awed them, till they stood
Quailing before her lion mood.
"You shrinking cowards!" foamed the Squire.

...the Squire took it upon himself...

To venture? Flora! - here, dog, here!"
At once the look of wrath was gone;
A trusting, tender, loving dawn
Rose in her eyes; her talking tail
Quivered with joy; a low soft wail
Broke from her, as the iron hand
Of the stout Squire from off her stand
Swung her; and striding towards the ledge
With his pleased burden, on the edge
Of awful death – oh, foul disgrace!
She turned and licked his purple face.
Sheer out he flung her. As she fell
Up from the palpitating hell

Came three shrill cries, and then a roll
Of thunder. Every pallid soul
Shrank from the pit; and ghastly white,

...what had they heard?...

Answer! What was it? – that last word
Which Flora flung me?" Answer came,
As though one mouth pronounced the name,
And smote the asker as a rod;
"The word she said was – 'God, God, God!'"

...the Squire, bedridden and overcome with grief...

Here they all come, the hellish pack,
Pouring from Cornwall Furnace, back
Into the world! Oh, see, see, see!
They snuff, to get the wind of me!

They've found it! Flora heads the whole

...finally driven by madness to his death...

Weak as I am, and like to die
Who must be hunted! With a bound
He reached the floor, and fled around.
Once, twice, thrice, round the room he fled,
Then in the nurses' arms fell dead.

...leaving behind a curse that lives on...

The Squire and all his race are gone;
But this wild legend still lives on.

Christ save us from the wretched fate
Of him who dared his wrath to sate
On God's dumb creatures, as of old
Befell the Squire of whom I told!

To this day, it is said the ghost of the tormented ironmaster still walks where the old Colebrook Furnace stood, with eyes glowing a fiery red, reflecting the horror of that day so long ago.

Ironmaster's house at Colebrook

A tragic horrifying end for a pack of faithful dogs... retribution in the form of eternal suffering for the wicked ironmaster...and for those who just happen to brush up against the evil that may still lurk at Colebrook...misfortune and suffering...

...Cursed

Shortly after the tormented demise of the Colebrook Furnace ironmaster, a series of tragedies struck the Robert Coleman family, and it seems, any one else who became involved with the facility. People began to wonder whether perhaps the "curse of the hounds" haunted one of the wealthiest families in America.

> **Robert Coleman**
> **1749 - 1825**
>
> Associate Judge of Lancaster County
> Member of Legislature
> Delegate to State Convention which
> Ratified the Constitution of
> the United States
> Ironmaster of Lancaster County
> Warden and Vestryman of St. James Church
> Father of Ann - Buried second memorial to right
> Ann was beloved of James Buchanan
> 15th President of the United States
> Also father of Sarah - Buried fifth memorial to right
> Sarah was beloved of Wm. Augustus Muhlenberg
> Co-Rector of St. James Church

Several Coleman children died while still in childhood, and two daughters reportedly committed suicide.

Robert Coleman's beautiful and high-strung 22-year-old daughter Ann fell in love with James Buchanan, who eventually became the fifteenth President of the United States. Ann and James were engaged and by all accounts adored each other. But Ann's father held a tainted opinion of her fiancé, and bitterly opposed Ann's relationship with Buchanan.

Although a successful and prosperous attorney highly thought of by his associates, James Buchanan had a few skeletons in his closet. While attending Dickinson College, Buchanan experienced disciplinary problems that almost thwarted his academic career. Robert Coleman, a member of the board at Dickinson, knew about Buchanan's troubles while attending school. Coleman felt that Buchanan did not measure up socially and suspected he might be gold-digging...hoping to acquire a part of his fortune through marriage.

When the chance to end the relationship between Ann and Buchanan arose, Coleman moved decisively. On returning from a business trip to Philadelphia, Buchanan stopped at his client's house to update him on the progress of his case. Innocently enough, Buchanan and the man's sister-in-law, there for a visit, engaged in a pleasant but brief conversation. That night, when Buchanan went to visit with Ann, she would not see him. Somehow, word had reached the Coleman household that Buchanan had first visited with another woman upon returning to Lancaster – a scandalous breach of moral decency by one engaged to marry. His attempts to explain were spurned, and he left unable to see her. Immediately, he wrote her a letter to clear the misunderstanding, but the letter came back - unopened. Ann, pressured by her parents to end the relationship, did so. In a letter to Buchanan, she broke off the engagement.

Heartbroken and reportedly still in love with Buchanan, Ann became depressed in the months following the episode. Her family became alarmed, and they arranged a visit to her sister in Philadelphia – a Christmas shopping trip that they hoped would cheer her up. During the visit, she declined several social invitations, preferring to stay in, alone. On one of those cold December nights, as midnight neared,

Ann committed suicide, reportedly from an overdose of opium and alcohol. Some believe she died from a broken heart.

The news devastated James Buchanan. Friends persuaded him to run for public office as a way to escape his grief. He did so, and from that moment on, he fashioned a brilliant political career culminating in the Presidency. But, James never married. He remained a bachelor his entire life, the only Presidential bachelor in our history. Reportedly, he carried Ann's picture with him always, and upon retiring to Wheatland, he had her picture mounted on the wall above his bed.

A short time later, the "curse" struck again. This time Ann's sister Sarah became a victim. Sarah fell in love with William Muhlenberg, Reverend of St. James Episcopal

> gray ladies: ghosts of women who...pined away for loss of love...haunt...because of their intense desire to be reunited with a loved one...
> - English folklore

Church, the same church that the Coleman family attended. Sarah unwittingly found herself in the middle of an intense feud between her father and

Muhlenberg over the scheduling of evening services. The conflict turned bitter and personal, and Robert Coleman so despised the young man that he forbade Sarah to marry him. But several years later when her father died, Sarah's life took a bittersweet twist.

She lost her beloved father, and with him the obstacle to marrying William disappeared...or so she thought.

Coleman family crypts at St. James Cemetery

Characteristically, the ever-shrewd Robert retained control, even from his grave. His will appointed Sarah's brother, who also despised Muhlenberg, as the administrator of her inheritance, and upon her marriage, Sarah's husband would not have any rights to Robert's substantial bequest. When Sarah learned of her father's spiteful last wishes, she became enraged and fled to Philadelphia where Sarah, too, took her own life.

William Muhlenberg left Lancaster after the church accepted an offer of $5,000 from the Coleman family to sever all ties with the Reverend. He, too, never married.

Following Robert Coleman's death, it appeared as if the curse abated, and the Coleman fortune continued to grow in the capable hands of Robert's four sons.

Thomas inherited the Colebrook Furnace, but he lived only to the age of 43, and by 1849 the legendary "furnace of the hounds" no longer played a vital role in the family's iron business. A soon-to-be-famous young man from Lancaster, John Reynolds of Civil War fame, took control of Colebrook Furnace. At the start of the war, Reynolds closed down the old iron factory, putting an end to the infamous furnace after 70 years of operation.

When all seemed to be forgotten, suddenly, the curse awakened.

A month later, Thomas, the 35-year-old son of William Coleman and head of the family fortune, unexpectedly passed away, and control transferred to his brother R.W.

> "Death Omen: whining of a dog beneath a window."
> - Superstitions of the Pennsylvania Germans

Two years later, John Reynolds fell on the battlefield at Gettysburg – a story told in another chapter in this book.

And the next year, R.W. perished unexpectedly at the relatively young age of 41.

The "curse of the hounds" struck with fury!

In a few short years, the entire Coleman empire, after generations of dominating the American iron industry and still one of the largest in the country, fell into the hands of William's children, nine-year-old Robert H. (called Bob) and seven-year-old Anne.

Bob Coleman would not escape the curse either.

The children were appointed a guardian, whom also managed the extensive family fortune, and in 1879 at just 23 years of age, Bob finally assumed full control of the vast estate. That same year he also married the lovely and passionate Lillie Clark, who he had met at college in Hartford, Connecticut.

> iron: ...protects against witches...but has little or no effect against ghosts...
> - English folklore

He also announced the re-opening of the Colebrook Furnace.

The newlyweds set off for Europe on a belated honeymoon, a trip with a dual purpose of purchasing furnishings for their new home – a magnificent mansion Bob had commissioned for completion upon their return.

But Lillie never saw that mansion completed. While in Italy, she fell sick and never recovered - the cause of death listed as "Roman Fever." Bob returned from his honeymoon alone, heartbroken and devastated. He had the mansion torn down and the stones were used to build the St. Luke's Episcopal Church in

Lebanon, Pennsylvania, where the body of Lillie lay interred beneath the altar of the church.

And again the "curse" fell silent...for a while.

Bob Coleman's mansion at Cornwall

Bob Coleman lost himself in his work. His business flourished, his fortune quadrupled, his wealth exceeded that of the other great industrialists of the time, J. P. Morgan and F. W. Vanderbilt. Bob remarried and raised a large family, living happily in the extravagant mansion at Cornwall Furnace.

But suddenly, the 100-year-old Coleman empire crumbled. Within a short period of time in the early 1890s, following several business misfortunes and miscalculations, the great majority of the Coleman wealth and holdings evaporated – gone to settle debts to creditors. Bob Coleman, the "Iron King of Pennsylvania," fell hard, and he lived out the rest of his life as a hermit in upstate New York.

After a century of almost continuous operation, the Colebrook Furnace lay silent, never to roar with fire again... never to betray innocent lives again...the end of the "curse of the hounds"...perhaps!

If you are at all superstitious, you might want to avoid that small town just north of Lancaster City...the town where they say you can still here the cry of the hunt on dark moonless nights...

THE CONESTOGAS

"IT WAS THE WORST OF TIMES, IT WAS A TURBULENT TIME"
PARAPHRASE OF CHARLES DICKENS 'A TALE OF TWO CITIES'

'INTO THE NIGHT' BY JOHNNY TIGER JR.

ON SUNDAY MORNING, DECEMBER 27TH 1763, THE PAXTON BOYS, A SELF
STYLED VIGILANTIC/MILITIA GROUP CAME TO THIS LOCATION
AND MURDERED THE REMAINING 14 MEMBERS OF THE COMMONLY REFERRED
TO CONESTOGA INDIANS. 13 DAYS PRIOR TO THIS THEY HAD MURDERED 6
OTHER MEMBERS OF THIS SMALL BAND.

TODAY WE ARE HONORED TO PAY OUR LAST RESPECTS TO THOSE
UNFORTUNATE SOULS WHO HAD BECOME REFUGEES IN THEIR OWN LAND.
THEY WERE NOT GUILTY OF ANY CRIME OTHER THAN BEING AT THIS PLACE
DURING THAT TURBULENT TIME.

THEY TOOK THAT FATEFUL JOURNEY INTO THE NIGHT.

SHEEHAYS (SHEHAES)	CHEE-NA-WAN (JACOB)
WASHEN (GEORGE)	QUAA-CHOW (YOUNG SHEHAES)
TEE-KAU-LEY (HARRY)	SHAW-E-KAH (A BOY)
ESS-CANESH (CAPT'N JOHN)	EX-UNDAS (A BOY CHRISLY)
TEAWONSHA-I-ONG (BETTY)	SAQ-UIES-HATTAH (CAPT'N JOHN'S SON)
KANNENQUAS (BILL SOCK)	TONG-QUAS (LITTLE PETER)
KYUNQUEAGOAH (MILLY SOCK)	HY-YE-NEAS (A BOY)
KOWEENASSE (JOHN SMITH)	KO-QUA-E-UN-QUAS (MOLLY)
TENSEEDAAGUA (PEGGY SMITH)	KAREN-DO-UAH (A LITTLE GIRL)
KANIINGUAS (LITTLE JOHN)	CANUKIE-SUNG (A LITTLE GIRL PEGGY)

UNTIL WE MEET AGAIN   FROM ALL OF US   JUNE 22,1997 AD

Bloody End

The Fulton Opera House stands on Prince Street as one of Lancaster City's crown jewels. But long before the theater existed, a horrific and bloody tragedy played out at that location. An act of horror that some people claim explains the reports of supernatural activity at the theater, reports that include an evil presence in the basement and mysterious visitors wandering the balcony.

In the mid-1700s, the Lancaster town jail occupied the site, and during that time, the last of a once plentiful tribe of Native Americans, the Conestogas, were bludgeoned to death, even as they sought sanctuary inside the walls of the jail. The horrendous, unjustified act of violence wiped out the few remaining members of the tribe, who became victims of barbaric vengeance carried out by local frontiersmen.

A recent archeological dig at the site uncovered ancient human bones that predate the massacre, suggesting that at one time it might also have served as a Native American burial ground. It does not take much of an imagination to understand why this area might be the most haunted in the entire city.

> Ghost Dance: ...a circle dance... intended to facilitate the return of the dead...
>
> – Native American custom

During the time of the French and Indian War, the Lancaster area existed on the outer edge of colonial civilization. The territory just beyond still belonged to the Native Americans, where the French were able to enlist the Indians in their struggle with England for control in the colonies. The conflict resulted in many savage raids with each side burning and pillaging the other's villages and settlements. The hostilities left many men, women and children dead on both sides.

Local settlers treated the Conestogas cautiously when they received word that Indian tribes in other parts of the colonies were causing trouble. But they knew that the Conestogas were peaceful and did not believe the Indians would turn to violence. They were a small tribe, decimated by centuries of disease and warfare. But there were other people outside the area with the notion that the Conestogas were dangerous savages, and they were determined to wage a war of genocide against the Native Americans.

In 1763, a group of vigilantes known as the "Paxton Boys" enforced their own brand of frontier justice on Indians and others throughout central Pennsylvania. In a paranoid strike against the small Conestoga Indian village just west of the town of

> meteors: ...the souls of the dead... coming to be reborn...
> - Native American folklore

Lancaster, the Paxton Boys killed six tribe members.

Fearing another attack, fourteen of the Conestogas, mostly women, children and old men, sought refuge inside the walls of the Lancaster town jail where they were allowed to stay under "protective custody."

But one Sunday in December, while many of the inhabitants of Lancaster were preoccupied with attending Christmas church services and the jail stood unprotected, the Paxton Boys snuck into town, forced their way into the jail and then murdered the defenseless refugees. The brutal attack all but wiped out the last of the Conestoga tribe.

William Henry, a nearby resident, witnessed the aftermath of the massacre and wrote a graphic account of the bloodbath, as he observed the broken and maimed bodies that cold December day:

> *"I ran into the prison yard, and there, O what a horrid sight presented itself to my view! Near the back door of the prison, lay an old Indian and his squaw, practically well known and esteemed by the people of the town, on account of his placid and friendly conduct.*
>
> *His name was Will Sock: across him and his squaw lay two children, of about the age of three years, whose heads were split with the tomahawk, and their scalps all taken off. Toward the middle of the jail yard...lay a stout Indian shot in the breast, his legs were chopped with the tomahawk, his hands cut off and finally a rifle ball discharged in his mouth.*
>
> *His head was blown to atoms, and the brains were splashed against, and yet hanging to the wall, for three or four feet around...In this manner lay the whole of them, men, women and children, spread about the prison yard: shot, scalped, hacked and cut to pieces."*

A section of the old jail still stands along the back of the Fulton Opera House along Water Street, as a memorial to the slaughter of those innocent victims. The limestone wall, preserved and incorporated in the existing structure, stands as a permanent reminder of the atrocities that took place at that site on perhaps the darkest day of Lancaster's history.

Old Jail Wall on Water Street

The news of the massacre spread throughout the colonies and Benjamin Franklin gave a moving criticism in his *Narrative of the Late Massacres in Lancaster County:*

"These Indians were the remains of a tribe of the Six Nations settled at Conestoga and thence called Conestoga Indians. On the first arrival of the English in Pennsylvania, messengers from this tribe came to welcome them, with presents of venison, corn, and skins; and the whole tribe entered into a treaty of friendship with the first proprietor, William Penn, which was to last as long as the sun should shine or the waters run in the rivers...

"If an Indian injures me, does it follow that I may revenge that injury on all Indians?... The only crime of these poor wretches seems to have been that they had a reddish-brown skin and black hair; and some people of that sort, it seems, had murdered some of our relations. If it be right to kill a man for such reason, then, should any man with a freckled face and red hair kill a wife or child of mine, it would be right for me to revenge it by killing all the freckled red-haired men, women, and children I could afterwards anywhere meet with...

"What had old Shehaes, so old he had been present at Penn's treaty in 1701, done that he should have been cut to pieces in his bed? What could he or the other poor old men and women do? What had little boys and girls done? What could children of a year old, babes at the breast, what could they do that they too must be shot and hatcheted? And in their parents' arms! This is done by no civilized nation in Europe. Do we come to America to learn and practice the manners of barbarians?... Unhappy people, to have lived in such times and by such neighbors!... In short, it would appear they would have been safe in any part of the known world except in the neighborhood of the Christian white savages of Peckstang and Donegal!"

Franklin's obvious contempt and disgust for the crime evokes heart-wrenching compassion for those so brutally murdered. Imagine the horror of it all. Men, women, children...the last of the Conestogas... gone forever.

Despite the uproar over the killings, the Paxton gang escaped retribution. They were not pursued...they were not arrested. They returned to their farms and villages, free to live their lives as if nothing happened.

At the time of the massacre, Matthias Slough operated the White Swan Inn at Penn Square on Queen Street. Edward Shippen, Esq., wrote a letter to the Governor on Dec. 27, 1763, saying "between two and three o'clock this afternoon upwards of a hundred armed men from the westward rode very fast into town, turned their horses into Mr. Slough's (an innkeeper's yard), and proceeded with the greatest precipitation to the work-house, where they stove open the door and killed all the Indians." As coroner, Slough also headed the inquest of the massacre that resulted in no action taken against the Paxton Boys. Matthias Slough is buried in the St. James Cemetery.

Is it any wonder that those innocent and defenseless Conestogas still haunt the ground where they were so savagely destroyed?

This story would not be complete without mention of one more incident that further compounded the awful tragedy.

The bodies were buried in a mass grave at the corner of Duke and Chestnut Streets (where a parking garage sits today) and the memory of the incident forgotten.

Forgotten, that is, until more than 50 years later, when a dig at the site for a new railroad turned up human bones. But progress was progress...and those old bones were in the way.

> ...Just before the Mexican-American War in 1846...came the description of the enemy as "mere Indians, barbarous savages," ...Twenty years before, Indians had had a higher status. But when New Jersey Sen. Theodore Frelinghuysen asked how the Indian Removal Act of 1830 could be justified under the Constitution, President Andrew Jackson declared, "They have neither the intelligence, the industry, the moral habits, nor the desire of improvement which are essential to any change in their condition. Established in the midst of another and superior race, they must necessarily yield to the force of circumstances, and erelong disappear."

In an era when attitudes toward the Native American people were still unenlightened, the bones were simply moved and reportedly reburied again, in an unmarked grave at St. James Church, just a block away.

And once again, those poor lost souls had no one to protect them...no one to bury them on their own land in their own sacred burial ground...no one to perform their elaborate burial ceremony and no one to provide a safe passage to their spiritual world where they could rest in peace. They were the last of their tribe. They were all alone...the forgotten dead!

Folks claim that the area on Duke Street between Orange and Chestnut Streets teems with ghostly figures that vanish into the shadows outside the library and along the walkways.

Is it any wonder that the spirits of those old men, women and children, victims of that terrible crime 250 years ago, betrayed in their quest for safety, are still with us, still wandering these streets...in their eternal quest for a lasting safe haven?

Within this churchyard rest in unmarked graves more than two hundred people: Townsfolk, Native Americans, Colonists, British and American Soldiers. These men, women and children, many of whom are unknown, represent the numerous religions, nationalities and races befriended by this parish in life and death.

This memorial is placed by St. James Church in sacred memory of these souls whose names, faith, love and deeds are known to God.

1985 A.D.

Phantoms in the Opera House

The "Phantom of the Opera" usually evokes haunting images of a deformed hermit that terrorizes the Paris Opera House. Lancaster's opera house has it's phantoms too – spectral visitors and mettlesome spirits that show no sign of a final performance anytime soon.

Built in 1852, the Fulton Opera House rose from the remnants of the city's pre-Revolutionary War jail at Prince Street, just a few doors north of King Street. A Lancaster businessman, Christopher Hager, hired the architectural firm of Sloan & Stewart to build what he planned as a community center. Somewhat reluctant to tear down the old jail, Hager left the back wall standing. Some say he incorporated the wall to honor the last of the Conestoga Indians, who met a tragic fate there so many years ago.

Originally known as Fulton Hall, it stood as the largest civic hall in Pennsylvania, and the brilliant history of the old theater parallels that of the American stage. "The Grand Old Lady of Prince

Street" showcased a number of prominent stars and acts through the years and became a showplace for many renowned performers such as Mark Twain, Buffalo Bill, John Phillip Sousa, and the illustrious Sarah Bernhardt, as well as numerous big-name shows that regularly graced her stage.

But unfortunately, as is the fate of many historical buildings, her grandness faded, and by 1963, a group formed to save the theater that others wanted to tear down. In 1969, the Fulton Opera House became a designated National Historic Landmark, a national treasure, and remains as a functioning playhouse.

However, history is not so clear when it comes to documenting the ghostly activities within the walls of this magnificent theater...ghosts that some say continue to perform, even though they departed this earth years ago!

Published in a variety of books, articles and pamphlets, the ghosts of the Fulton seem to perform as much as the artists who have graced her stage. The stories are told regularly on the *Ghosts of Lancaster*, a candlelight walking tour in town. And after hearing additional tales from customers on the tour who have had their own experiences while visiting the Fulton, plans were made for a private tour of the Opera House, where the storytellers could witness the setting for these tales with their own eyes. Following are the experiences of the tour takers.

Playwright-In-Residence and Family Theater Director, Barry Kornhauser, agreed to the tour, and he proved to be a most gracious, although somewhat skeptical, host. Walking through the doors of the four-story theater is like walking into a palace. Deep reds and brilliant golds enhance the plush Victorian interior. Gently rising staircases provide the perfect backdrop for a scene from *Cinderella* or *Gone With the Wind*. If you had to pick one word to describe the Fulton, that word would have to be "elegant."

After introductions and a brief view of the lobby, Mr. Kornhauser immediately ushered everyone to the lowest level of the theater. Not dark and dreary, as one might imagine, the area shines brightly - except for one wall. A dark stone wall surrounding the old wooden jail door looms in testament to that dark Sunday morning in 1763 when the last of the Conestoga Indians were massacred. Next to the old entrance way hangs a plaque listing the names of those who lost their lives that day.

In this room, according to Mr. Kornhauser, many employees complain of an uncomfortable feeling, as if someone watches them. "It's almost as if you feel someone is going to walk up behind you and say something, but if you turn around, there's no one there," he said. On a recent visit to the Fulton, a Native American now living in Canada said that he could clearly sense the "energy" of the murdered Indians a few yards west of the spot, in what was the theater's old green room. In addition, during an excavation some years ago, ancient human bones were unearthed, leading some to believe that the site could have been a Native American burial ground, prior to the construction of the prison in the early 1700s.

As the group moved upstairs, a lighter mood prevailed, and everyone agreed that it felt as though a "heaviness" had lifted. Walking onto the stage, Mr. Kornhauser began to recreate the ghostly scenes that have played out before so many. Taking a deep breath and with a sweeping gesture across the stage, he began, "It's said that there are many spirits in this area."

candles: in the superstition of the theater...three candles are never to be lit in the dressing room.

Pointing up to scaffolding, some 70 feet above, Mr. Kornhauser continued, "There are supposedly two spirits up there. On the scaffolding is a female presence that many describe as cold and frightening. And just below her, on the pinrail, exists a warm and friendly presence. We don't have a clue who they could be or why they haunt up there, but many have felt them."

Moving to the center of the stage, Mr. Kornhauser continued by saying that people often feel gusts of cold air and see lights mysteriously go off and then on again - typical of what one might associate with a haunted building. But there are other more chilling events that occur with no explanation. "The stage manager is usually the last person to leave, responsible for turning off lights and locking doors. On several occasions, upon returning the next morning, chairs and furniture would be tossed about and lights turned on. Once an entire audience witnessed a weird and unexplainable incident. During a final performance just before the theater closed for renovations, on the last note of a piano concert, the ivory from one of the keys flew off the piano as a light exploded overhead!"

Various casts also experienced the supernatural: "Many actors and actresses have reported seeing a white mist approach the stage as it travels down the center of the theater, up to the orchestra pit, and then disappears. It happens during performances, causing the actors to jumble their lines now and then." Kornhauser explained that up until 1904, the theater had a center aisle, instead of the two off-center aisles of today, leading many to believe that the entity returns from before that time...perhaps some poor soul searching for a seat!

One of the best-known ghostly visitors to the Fulton, appropriately enough dubbed the "woman in white," may be a long ago actress. As Mr. Kornhauser explained, "A woman in a white dress often appeared on the old stage stairway. When one of our crewmembers approached the elegant lady, she said her name was Marie, and then she gradually disappeared down the steps." An inspection of the theater archives revealed that an actress by the name of Marie Cahill performed regularly at the Fulton around the turn of the century. She had a reputation for being strong-willed and rarely took a role where she did not wear her trademark white dress. "We don't know why she haunts here," said Mr. Kornhauser. "But, ironically, Marie was born the year the Fulton converted from a meetinghouse to a theater. She died some 60 years later, in 1933, the same year that the theater stopped doing plays and converted to showing movies." Does Marie continue in some kind of eternal performance...maybe still perfecting her act?

Leaving the stage, Mr. Kornhauser led the small group up the stairway to the balcony where a spectacular view of the stage appeared. Added in 1904 and known as the Peanut Gallery or Peanut

Heaven, the second balcony provides an intimate view of the stage, and, as Mr. Kornhauser pointed out, perhaps a phantom or two. "Behind the seating

area and behind this wall, is a space where the technicians work. Many of them hear footsteps and have eerie feelings of being watched. Customers in these seats have described the same sensations."

The Peanut Gallery also provided Mr. Kornhauser with his very own "supernatural" experience that left him a little less doubtful...if not a completely convinced believer. "We were rehearsing a play. The house was dark, but we did have the stage lights on. All of a sudden a light appeared in the Peanut Gallery. Looking up to see where this light was coming from, we then saw the emergency crash doors up here begin banging, open then closed, again and again. We ran up here and didn't find anyone. We even opened the emergency doors and there was no one outside, except the people gathered down at the street wondering who was banging the doors from the inside!"

As the tour ended, no one wanted to leave. Not just because of the theater's charming atmosphere, but also for a chance performance...perhaps by the mysterious "lady in white."

Note:

During the summer of 2000, on the Ghosts of Lancaster, PA walking tour, a local Lancaster businessperson shared her story of an eerie experience she had while attending a

children's piano recital at the Fulton. As she told it, "A group of us parents and kids were climbing the stairs, and we noticed a pool of blood on one of the steps. We ushered the kids away and found a custodian. When we got back we couldn't believe our eyes. There wasn't a thing there...no mark...no moisture...nothing."

Another tidbit, heard on the ghost tour in 1998: the Fulton hosted several Native American tribes who came to "cleanse" the Fulton. Each tribe performed their own unique burial ritual to help any lost spirits find their way to the "spirit land." However, since the 14 massacred people were the last of the Conestogas, speculation exists that the ceremonies were not conducted according to tribal traditions, thus rendering the rites of passage unsuccessful.

Mrs. Penn's Shoppe in Strasburg and
starting point for the ghost tour.

Tales of Strasburg

The Ghosts of Lancaster, PA, a candlelight walking tour, began offering tours in Strasburg in 1997. Many of the tales were originally based on newspaper articles and various publications that covered reports of haunted activity throughout the entire Pennsylvania Dutch area, from the hills of the Blue Mountains to the farms of Paradise. Within a short period of time, many of Strasburg's inhabitants came forward with their own stories of supernatural activity in town, replacing most of the out-of-town stories. In the last seven years, many more details, mostly from customers on the tour, have surfaced that add much to the tales of ghosts, spirits and apparitions said to be haunting Strasburg.

The noise of passing trucks and cars, as well as the commotion of tourists strolling its streets, certainly places Strasburg in the 21st century. But the occasional clip-clop of the Amish buggy passing through town recalls a simpler time, when this Main Street was the *main* thoroughfare between Lancaster and Philadelphia, commonly referred to as the Conestoga Road. Early settlers of the 18th century used it on their way to the western frontier, sharing the well-traveled route with the merchants who carried goods to the inhabitants and trading ships at the port in Philadelphia.

Strasburg at dusk.

Strasburg slowly developed into a town from the time Swiss Mennonites built the first houses in the area in 1733. For a period of time, the fledgling village carried the name of Hell's Hole because of the impoverished condition of its inhabitants and the considerable number of taverns that lined the road through town. For a while, Beggartown became a hardly less flattering moniker, until its shabby log dwellings were replaced by more substantial structures containing churches, schools and businesses. Eventually, the town took on a more civilized look, and in 1816, adopted the name Strasburg, named after the town Strasbourg, France.

All the stories in the book from this point on are part of the ghost tour in Strasburg...a town that time forgot...where the dead walk with the living and lurk in the shadows of a place that is truly ***haunted!***

Strasburg Cemetery

Of all the stops on the ghost tour, the Strasburg Cemetery ranks as everyone's favorite...and why not? A classic, iron-fenced, monument laden field of ancient tombstones, with a big old bat-infested tree in the center, makes an excellent location for telling ghost stories.

Situated behind the Presbyterian Church at the corner of Decatur and Franklin Streets, many of Strasburg's long ago residents rest in peace there, and have done so for hundreds of years. But some are not so peaceful...or restful! Based on firsthand encounters of the "mysterious kind" as experienced on the ghost tour, many people consider the cemetery the scariest place in town.

On the same night in 1999, four people split across two tours claimed to see the misty form of a woman pass behind the large tombstone to the left of the big tree. One happened to be a psychic, and she thought the phantom woman's name started with an "M."

Barb, a very levelheaded tour guide, witnessed the

ghostly figure of a man near the entrance gate, as he walked behind her tour group. Well-dressed in a suit, carrying a briefcase and *headless*, he crossed the walkway and disappeared. Shortly thereafter, Barb quit giving tours.

Hi, my name is Jim Evans. I took your tour on Saturday April 19th. I took pictures of the tombstone in the graveyard while I was there with my digital camera and when I got home and printed everything out that picture was not there. I made a menu from the camera that gives you a preview and a number of all the pictures stored on the camera. The picture is not there either and the numerical counter goes from #58 to #60. I don't know what happened to #59, it just isn't there. The tour guide (Nora) told us that if anything strange happened while we were on the tour we could let you know. I just thought I would pass on the information.

– email 2003

In 2000, longtime tour guide Joy had an unusual experience that disrupted her ghost tour. While under the big tree on a dark October evening with the ground covered in leaves, she reached a suspenseful point in her story, when suddenly the leaves swirled in a whirlwind directly in front of her surprised listeners, rose in the air and fell to the ground. Several people let out screams and several others hurried out the cemetery gates to wait for the rest of the group.

Another tour guide, Eileen, observed two customers as they experienced their own close encounter midway through her story. As the group huddled underneath the tree, one woman quickly turned and looked over her shoulder. A couple of minutes later, the same woman and the woman next to her quickly turned and looked again. The obviously perplexed duo glanced at each other and shrugged their shoulders. While walking out of the cemetery, the first woman asked Eileen if she could talk to her after the tour. When the tour concluded shortly thereafter, the woman said that she had a weird experience in the cemetery. She felt a tap on her shoulder while listening to Eileen's story and initially thought her husband wanted her. But he had moved to the other side of the group to smoke a cigarette. When the tap came again, she glimpsed the almost transparent head and shoulders of a woman with a "Gibson girl" look - hair pulled up and a high lace

Old, bat-infested tree

collar. Then the spectral figure disappeared. She felt that the woman next to her might also have seen it, as they both turned to look at the same time. Coincidently, Eileen ran into the other woman while in the Creamery a short time later, and she described the same experience - the two women did not know each other.

One clear dark night, as Nora stopped her group under the tree, the beam of light from her flashlight illuminated a mist that hung in the air for a minute or so, and then disappeared. Everybody saw the ethereal fog, but nobody could explain it.

Yes indeed, strange things happen in that cemetery.

And perhaps the strangest of all involves one of Strasburg's legendary ghost stories.

> "If a bat flies into your house it is a sure sign the devil is after you."
> -Superstitions of the Pennsylvania Germans

On Main Street in Strasburg sits one of the town's most unique homes, a twin-turreted, nearly 100-year-old mansion. Its uniqueness extends beyond the physical, however, for the old Gonder Mansion holds the distinction of harboring one of the best known, and often told, legends in all of Lancaster County.

The legend, repeated in several books and numerous publications, typically concerns only the particulars of the eye-catching structure's history, and the sad relationship between the individuals who lived there – and wanted to live there. But other mysteries connect the legend of the Gonder Mansion to the Strasburg Cemetery as well.

The story begins with the completion of the magnificent building in 1905 by B.B. Gonder, who made his fortune in the railroad industry during the boom times of the late 1800s. Up to that point, B.B. and his family, along with his spinster sister Annie, lived in the comparatively small home next door to the property where B.B. built the mansion. According to legend, the trouble started when the Gonder family moved into the stately and opulent estate.

B.B. left his sister Annie behind. With his wife and

Scowling stuccoed face!

their two children, he moved into the splendid new home, but Annie remained in the old, small house — in the shadow of the mansion. Some speculate that a feud raged between Annie and B.B., or Annie and B.B.'s wife, causing her ostracism. Some people say that the weird faces built into the stucco with pieces of mirror just under the eaves, two smiling and one frowning, are proof of the discord between them.

Whatever the issues were in their relationship so long ago no one knows, but several years after the new arrangement, Annie reportedly suffered from melancholia and unexpectedly left town, only to commit suicide by drowning herself in the Pequea Creek just outside Strasburg.

The legend goes on to say that Annie, never allowed to live in the lovely mansion, spends her afterlife there, haunting the corridors and parlors of the home denied her. Apparently, Annie only haunts the men who live in the house, since they are the only ones that hear the cackling laugh of a woman or glimpse the ghostly image of an old lady flitting about. Five men, including B.B. Gonder, are said to have died in the mansion. Maybe Annie found a way to get even with her brother, by exacting an everlasting revenge.

Perhaps clues exist at the Strasburg Cemetery to indicate who truly laughed last.

As you enter the cemetery through the iron-gate on Franklin Street and walk towards the big tree in the center of the cemetery, just before that tree, off to the right, sits the Gonder family burial plot. Aligned in a neat row are the tombstones of B.B., his wife,

Mystery of the Tombstones

their children and several other family members. But no Annie! Oh, Annie's tombstone is there, but hers faces away from the others, positioned behind her family – cast out *once again.*

Now, you might suspect that B.B. had something to do with the graveyard arrangement, as you might suspect he had something to do with the living arrangement. But careful inspection of the dates on the tombstones reveals that B.B., taken suddenly by a heart-attack, preceded Annie to the grave.

Perhaps B.B.'s wife, Mary, who survived them both, made the final decision on the burial plot arrangements. Could it be that Annie and her sister-in-law were at odds, unable to live under the same roof? Maybe Annie, stung and humiliated by her treatment at the hands of her brother, in a final act of spite, chose her own burial location away from the family that spurned her.

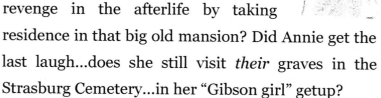

Again no one really knows. But, could dear old Annie have found eternal revenge in the afterlife by taking residence in that big old mansion? Did Annie get the last laugh...does she still visit *their* graves in the Strasburg Cemetery...in her "Gibson girl" getup?

Ghost Tour Update:

One night following the ghost tour, a man introduced himself to the tour guide as a member of the family that lived in the mansion after the Gonders. He shared several fascinating details that might add to the legend. Both of his parents passed away in the mansion, his father at the top of the back stairs and his mother in the front parlor.

A man and woman who have visited Strasburg regularly for over 40 years, and took the ghost tour, wondered whether they might have seen Annie or some other ghost. In the 1970s while visiting town, renovations were underway on the mansion, and out of curiosity, the couple climbed the porch steps to peer into the windows. They saw an old woman in a rocking chair in the front parlor but she never acknowledged their presence, despite their knocking on the door and windows to get her attention.

Digital photograph of a misty form at Annie's tombstone, taken by John Berkenbush during the ghost tour.

Hell's Tunnel

While visiting the Pennsylvania Dutch Country, one of the most enjoyable pastimes is a leisurely drive through the rolling countryside. The stress that so often accompanies day-to-day activities slowly fades away along the winding roads surrounded by verdant farmland. Sometimes, though, visitors get lost out on those lonely back roads. Every cornfield looks like the last one, the hills are indistinguishable...each farm stands in solitude.

So, while exploring, keep this old (and simple) way of navigating in the back of your mind. The roads leading out of Lancaster are like fingers on a hand - the city being the palm and the main roads such as Route 30 and 741 are fingers. The side roads run perpendicular to the main roads, almost forming a grid. In other words, should you get lost on a back road, first of all: DON'T PANIC! YOU ARE IN LANCASTER COUNTY! Second: just keep going. You will eventually get to a main road.

Traveling these back roads, the scenes are timeless — Amish buggies, barefoot children, farmers plowing - simple scenes. But so simple it takes a moment to register in your brain that this is here...this is now. This is the draw of the Dutch County - simplicity - the feeling of stepping back in time.

However, one road is deceivingly tranquil...and if you are unlucky enough to find your way onto it, and your heart starts pounding and you get the feeling that you really should turn around... perhaps you should heed that warning!

> crossroads: ...at midnight on New Year's Eve, the dead can be conjured to appear by standing within the rectangle formed by horse-cart tracks at a crossroads...the ghost will appear when its name is called...and will answer three questions...
> -Danish folklore

According to locals, a few miles south of the Center Square of Strasburg near the Little Beaver Creek, exists a mysterious place they call Hell's Tunnel. As the legend goes, unsuspecting travelers have turned down that secluded and deserted road, a dead-end road, never to return!

Unlike the wide-open, sun drenched farmland thoroughfares, the narrow tree-lined Sides Mill Road winds through a claustrophobic passageway squeezed between a rocky creek on one side and a

steep hill looming on the other. The canopy of trees reaching up and over the lane creates an illusion of traveling through a tunnel - a dark tunnel of branches and leaves.

As the dimly shadowed passageway of macadam turns into

Hell's Tunnel?

dirt and gravel, the road disappears at a tree-covered embankment, and nestled in a grove of thick trees and undergrowth sits the more than 200-year-old Sides Mill.

Early records show that in 1762, Samuel and Agnes Hawthorne held a mortgage for 320 acres that included the site, making it one of the oldest surviving mills in Lancaster County. The mill itself appeared on the tax rolls in 1792. Somewhat unusual for Lancaster County, the mill contained living quarters for the miller, his family and the workers, all housed beneath one roof. Stone and frame structures were added over the years, and milling continued until 1936, when the mill ceased operating. Reportedly, the doors were locked and it remained untouched for decades. And since that time, an eerie mystique surrounded the abandoned mill spawning weird stories of lost travelers and unexplained sightings.

Apparently, rumors started when unsuspecting motorists stumbled upon the dead-end road, and discovered the old isolated mill at the end of the lane. Some claimed that they saw a face at the front window. It only appeared for an instant – and disappeared at the blink of an eye. The face glowed with a green tint, and word spread that the old mill was haunted. The story passed down from generation to generation, and a "right of passage" for local teens involved a stealthy adventure to catch a glimpse of the "green-faced ghost." Invariably, the neophyte ghost hunters would tell the story of approaching the darkened mill and the sudden appearance of the green-faced ghost at its door – frightening them off.

The local legend was told by Bill, a customer on the ghost tour in the summer of 1998. He shared the story with the

> "A person born in January can see ghosts."
> - Superstitions of the Pennsylvania Germans

entire group, and so captivated the audience with his vivid descriptions and details of the abandoned mill, as well as the creepy road leading to it, that the tour guide, Eileen, asked Bill whether he would take her there after the tour ended. Several others asked to come along and at about 11:30 p.m., a mini-caravan of vehicles started out of Strasburg for the haunted mill.

First though, Bill gave some advice, "Follow closely, and if I get frightened, I'm turning around and leaving– so it's every man for himself."

As the witching hour approached, the cars wound their way slowly down the twisting, abandoned road, with their headlights poking through the black tunnel formed by the overhanging trees that wrapped the small party of ghost hunters in darkness. Bill slowed to a halt, and the old stone mill loomed in the shadows on the left. The only sound came from the trickle of water that, at one time, turned the giant wheel of the mill. With their headlights off and completely surrounded in darkness, the small party scanned the doorways and windows of the old mill for the green glowing figure. After several minutes of nervous apprehension in the perfect stillness of midnight, alone in the middle of nowhere chasing apparitions became too much for the imagination, and the spooked party of ghost-seekers turned around and headed out of "Hell's Tunnel," ending their night of exploration.

Some people claim that a murder took place in the mill, and the victim's avenging soul appears as the glowing figure. But perhaps, the tragic accident in 1936 that ended the structure's days as a mill, and also the life of the structure's namesake, Aldus Sides, who perished when he became entangled in the water wheel, explains the mysterious sightings at the old mill.

As for the fate of the historic Sides Mill, a suspicious fire on July 25, 1999 left much of the mill in ruins, but the old stone skeleton remains...and perhaps, a glowing green ghost!

Ghost Tour Update:

Sightings of several other apparitions along Sides Mill Road have been reported. Soldiers appear in the woods opposite the creek side of the road, and a young woman dressed in a flowing white dress appears suddenly on the roadway, but as the car seemingly hits her, the ghostly figure disappears.

Mrs. Yates

Although most people do not recognize the name Gilbert Stuart, they are familiar with his artwork. Stuart painted the portraits of many of our country's colonial-era dignitaries, including the picture of George Washington that graces the one-dollar bill. He also painted a picture of Mrs. Yates, a print of which hangs in perhaps the area's finest hotel and restaurant, the Historic Strasburg Inn. And although Mrs. Yates' obscure reputation *pales* in comparison to Washington's, encounters with the haggish-looking woman have caused more than one person to turn *pale* in fright.

Mrs. Yates' picture, along with many other colonial-era pictures, adorns the walls of the lovely Inn, but Mrs. Yates seems to get all the blame when it comes to the alleged unexplained phenomenon that occurs.

The story first came to light in 1998, when a couple on the Ghost Tour wondered whether the Historic Strasburg Inn might be haunted. The couple heard strange noises while staying there, and they were certain the place must be haunted. Eileen, their tour guide, became intrigued by their tale and decided to investigate, hoping to find another ghost story for the tour...and boy did she hit the jackpot. Mrs. Yates proved to be as unpredictable and frightening as the couple said.

Nestled on a beautiful stretch of farmland, the Historic Strasburg Inn and the several buildings that comprise the facility provide the perfect setting for an Amish-country stay. Centrally located just off Route 896 on the way into Strasburg, the Inn is within a short drive of all the major attractions and shopping outlets.

The long, street lamp lined driveway leading up to the stately structure gives the feeling of stepping back in time. It very much resembles an inn that might have existed 200 years ago. In addition to the Inn's accommodations, there are two fine restaurants, the elegant Washington House Restaurant and the By George Tavern...certainly, one of Lancaster County's finer establishments... despite Mrs. Yates' occasional antics.

Knowing that some places of business are reluctant to share stories of alleged hauntings, a few discreet inquiries were made at the front desk. The question, "Is this place haunted?" caused the desk clerk to make a few furtive glances around the room before whispering, "I think so."

Historic Strasburg Inn

The young man then went on to explain how guests hear voices, disembodied voices, in the Washington House Restaurant, and many of the employees also experience strange noises and eerie sightings. A young woman from behind the desk joined the conversation, "Quite often when I'm working here, I'll catch a shadow out of the corner of my eye, but when I turn to look, nothing's there. It happens over and over, as if someone...or something...almost wants to be noticed. It really gives me the willies." With a shiver she added, "Go talk to Anne, she works in the Washington House dining room where lots of *stuff* happens."

The waitress, busy setting tables for the fast approaching dinner hour, jumped at the inquiring "Anne?" from her visitors. After brief introductions, Anne acknowledged that "yes indeed, strange things happen here."

In a hushed tone, even though no one else could hear, and pointing to a picture hanging on the wall, she said softly, "It's her. She doesn't want us to be here. We're used to it, but the feeling is always here, as if we're not welcome."

From the picture, an old, dour, angular-faced woman stares from underneath an old fashioned bonnet. Mrs. Yates' unnerving gaze from her position on the wall, as if ignoring everything else but *you*...as if she can actually see *you* from inside that picture, while pretending to sew, is hauntingly surreal.

Anne continued, no longer in a hushed tone, "Sometimes we hear the murmur of a woman's voice, the words are indistinguishable. The guests hear it too...a voice right next to them. But the weirdest thing happened a couple of years ago."

Anne described how early one morning, as she prepared the dining room for the morning breakfast crowd, a woman approached her quite cautiously. Anne noted that the woman looked very uncomfortable and wore a rather ill-fitting, mismatched outfit and nervously asked, "Is this place haunted?"

The woman, a member of a women's association staying at the hotel, went on to explain that the night before, she had laid her clothing on a chair next to the bed. The following morning her clothes were not where she left them, but on the floor, she saw a puddle of water with wet footsteps leading to the bathroom. In the bathroom, her clothes were draped over the side of the tub, soaking wet, as if someone had washed them! Of course, she immediately questioned her roommate, or rather, accused her. But her surprised roommate knew nothing about it. The bewildered woman concluded, "Either someone came into our room and did this while we both slept, or this place is haunted!"

Anne chuckled as she told the story, but immediately reverted back to a more serious tone and suggested, "Laura, in the tavern, has some stories. You should talk to her."

"bean-nighe" A banshee-like wraith that appears most often in the Highlands as an ugly and frightening female figure washing bloody grave clothes in anticipation of an impending death.
                    -Scottish Folklore

Laura, standing behind the bar while preparing the cash drawer for the evening's business, readily stepped aside to chat. She had a warm and confident personality and made it clear that she did not frighten easily. As tavern manager, her job requires that she close up at night, usually the last person to leave, which does not bother her.

"However," Laura stated, "Some nights I get a strong feeling that I shouldn't be here. Like everyone else, I blame it on Mrs. Yates." Laura went on to explain that the rooms in the Inn are named after people with some connection to the property. Except nobody knows what connection Mrs. Yates has, or why her picture hangs in the dining room. "The picture is never straight, as soon as you straighten it, the next time you pass the darned thing, it's crooked again," explained Laura. "There's a lovely fireplace in that room, but some nights we can't keep the flames going. It's a gas fireplace, and we've had it checked, but it constantly goes out and needs relighting."

Laura also blames Mrs. Yates for the mischief that occurs with the doors. "As the other employees leave, I lock the doors to each section. For some reason, as I pass by a section I just locked a few minutes ago, the doors will be wide open."

Laura recalled one evening in particular that spooked her. "I was doing my totals for the night in the tavern. Everyone had left except Jessica. She offered to go upstairs and make sure all the lights were out. In a few moments, she was back in the tavern and asked me what I wanted. Just as I began to tell her that I hadn't called her, we both heard a woman's voice, which surprised us, because no else should have been there."

Laura continued, "I told Jessica we should check upstairs, maybe a customer got locked in. Jessica went up the back stairs, and I went up the front. We didn't find anyone, but as we got back here we heard a woman's mumbled voice again, followed by the sound of a man's voice. We left immediately."

The concerned look on Laura's face lightened up as she recalled another incident. "A woman came into the tavern and asked me if the place was haunted, because something very strange had occurred in her room. During the night, she woke up to use the bathroom. There she found her robe lying across the toilet, and she swore that she left it on her suitcase when she went to bed. She also noticed that the floor and shower stall were wet - as if someone had taken a shower and intended to use the robe when they were through! She asked to be moved to another room."

Laura had no reason to think that Mrs. Yates might be behind any of the incidents, other than she felt certain that a woman's spirit haunts the inn and the unusual reaction most people have to her picture. In an uncertain joking tone she said, "Maybe Mrs. Yates was a teetotaler and doesn't approve of alcohol!"

Research into the history of the property turned up no mysterious deaths, accidents, calamities or tragic love stories that could explain the alleged haunting of the Historic Strasburg Inn. The question of who or why remains a mystery, but perhaps, as some people think, a connection exists between Mrs. Yates and Strasburg that might explain the restless spirit that seemingly haunts this area of Strasburg.

We know that Catherine Brass Yates lived from 1755 to 1828 and married the senior partner in the New York firm of Yates & Pollock, importers of East Indian and European goods. Perhaps Mrs. Yates traveled to Strasburg with her husband on a business trip to Lancaster. After all, the Conestoga Road, a major trading route, passed through town, and the popular Washington Hotel sat at the intersection of present day Routes 741 and 896. Or, perhaps her portrait by the famed Gilbert Stuart and the peculiar penetrating stare he captured provides enough celebrity for Mrs. Yates' picture to hang in the Historic Strasburg Inn.

The old Washington Hotel stood at the square in Strasburg from at least 1793 until demolished in 1964. Some of the old relics and keepsakes from that historic structure ended up in the Historic Strasburg Inn, built in 1973. Could one of these relics be from Mrs. Yates' time? Perhaps even owned by Mrs. Yates...maybe a favorite item of hers. Perhaps the combination of her picture and one of her personal items from so long ago is enough to connect Mrs. Yates to the here and now.

However, when you visit this jewel of Strasburg to enjoy a wonderful meal, a few drinks or a relaxing stay in the country, carefully check out the odd look in Mrs. Yates' eye, and see if you feel as if she actually watches *you*!

Ghost Tour Update:

A staff-member reported activity on the top floor of the Washington House. People claim to see a woman in the window on the end of the building – in a room never used.

Who's at the window?

After hearing the story of Mrs. Yates, one customer thanked the tour guide for clearing up a rather dicey situation that occurred between him and his wife. Apparently, while they were staying at the Inn with another couple, the women went shopping and the men visited the trains. Upon returning, the man's wife found a foreign tube of lipstick on their bed – raising some uncomfortable questions on her part. Mrs. Yates seemed the most likely explanation to him.

The original portrait of Mrs. Yates hangs in the National Gallery of Art in Washington, D.C. Gilbert Stuart's reputation as a "vain and hard-drinking" artist did not stop the famous from posing. Despite his liquored breath, a sharp wit and outstanding skill made the discomfort worthwhile. His Philadelphia studio once stood at Fifth and Chestnut Streets, next to the Library Company Building in the area of the Signer's Garden, reportedly a well-known haunted site.

"Damn pretty as ever!"

Reportedly, apparitions appear in the vicinity of 101 East Main Street in Strasburg. At one time Echternach's Hotel operated at the site, offering its patrons a unique amenity – a bar situated in such a way that a horse rider could be served without dismounting.

According to a Mrs. Ferguson, one day a stranger named Wharton arrived in town with bulging saddlebags, fell in love with one of Echternach's daughters and married her. As it turns out, Wharton had a criminal past and when the authorities caught up to him and arrested him Wharton's marriage also ended. Eventually, Echternach's daughter remarried and moved to Philadelphia, where one day as she strolled along Chestnut Street, a man approached and said to her, "Damn pretty as ever!" He looked vaguely familiar to her, but he promptly disappeared, never to be seen again.

Some people wonder whether Echternach's daughter encountered a ghost that day in Philadelphia and if it might not be the same spirit haunting Main Street in Strasburg.

Old Jake's demise

Old Jake

This story came about in a rather unusual manner. Well into the first year of running the ghost tour in Strasburg, a letter came in the mail. Typically, letters to the ghost tour take one of several forms: requests for information on scheduling and cost, letters from customers who have enjoyed the tour, and occasionally, a ghost story. This one-page, manually typed letter, signed simply "D," did contain a ghost story, one that the writer claims originates from Strasburg. Perhaps it does. Some ghost stories are generic enough that they could occur anywhere, and sometimes folklore gets a little confusing when trying to pinpoint the exact location of a particular legend.

The letter started out with compliments to the ghost tour, as the writer had taken the tour and thoroughly enjoyed the experience, and further more, as a staff member of the Pennsylvania Dutch Convention & Visitor's Bureau, would surely recommend the tour to visitors and locals alike. However, the letter-writer had one complaint and wanted to bring it to our attention. A very old Strasburg ghost story, part of the folklore of the small town for over a century, did not get mentioned.

How many of you are familiar with the saying, "I'll be there with bells on"? According to the letter, it is an old-time saying that originated in Strasburg, as a boast by wagon-masters concerning their skills at successfully navigating the treacherous roadways! And, according to the letter, those old-time bells can still be heard ringing in Strasburg.

The early roads in Pennsylvania were not easy to navigate. Not only did travelers have to wind their way up and down, over and around the contour of the land, but farmers also fenced their land, forcing travelers on zigzag routes from town to town. These "roads" were nothing more than earthen trails that became virtually impassable anytime it rained. The main route to and from Philadelphia (the great market to the east) in Colonial times, the Conestoga Road, fell into this category, and one report described it as "Liable to continued alterations... almost impassable for want of Repair."

EARLY TRANSPORTATION ROUTES

KING STREET

THROUGHOUT LANCASTER CITY'S HISTORY, KING STREET HAS BEEN A MAJOR THOROUGHFARE BETWEEN PHILADELPHIA AND POINTS WEST. IN 1733 WORK COMMENCED ON THE KING'S HIGHWAY, NOW ROUTE 340. THIS HIGHWAY BEGAN AT THE SQUARE, EXTENDED EASTWARD ON KING STREET AND CONTINUED ON TO PHILADELPHIA. ALTHOUGH THE HIGHWAY IMPROVED TRAVEL BETWEEN LANCASTER AND PHILADELPHIA, THE DIRT ROADBED BECAME IMPASSABLE IN INCLEMENT WEATHER. IN 1792 THE STATE CHARTERED THE PHILADELPHIA-LANCASTER TURNPIKE COMPANY WHICH BUILT THE PHILADELPHIA-LANCASTER TURNPIKE, A PART OF THE PRESENT-DAY U.S. 30 AND THE FIRST TURNPIKE IN THE UNITED STATES. THE NEW ROUTE WAS CONSTRUCTED WITH A HARD, MACADAM SURFACE, MAKING IT PASSABLE YEAR ROUND.

UNFORTUNATELY, KING STREET ITSELF WAS NOT SURFACED, AND CONTINUED TO BE DUSTY IN DRY WEATHER AND A SEA OF MUD IN WET WEATHER. TO AVOID TAXING CITIZENS FOR PAVING THE STREET, LANCASTER RECEIVED PERMISSION FROM THE STATE LEGISLATURE TO HOLD A LOTTERY TO RAISE $20,000. THE DRAWING TOOK PLACE ON MAY 1, 1802: FIRST PRIZE WAS $1,000, WITH SECOND PRIZE BEING $500; MORE THAN FOUR THOUSAND OTHER PRIZES WERE AWARDED. ON MAY 28TH, PAVING BEGAN FROM THE CONESTOGA RIVER EXTENDING WESTWARD TO THE SQUARE.

IN ORDER TO ACCOMMODATE TRAVELLERS, STAGECOACHES LEFT LANCASTER FOR POINTS EAST AND WEST. IN THE MID-EIGHTEENTH CENTURY, A TRAVELLER GOING TO PHILADELPHIA WOULD CATCH MATTHIAS SLOUGH'S DISPATCH STAGE LINE AT THE WHITE SWAN HOTEL AT 5:00 A.M. AND WOULD ARRIVE IN PHILADELPHIA THAT EVENING.

In the early 1700s, as the city of Philadelphia and surrounding settlements grew rapidly, so did the demand for food. The rich farmland of rural Lancaster provided plentiful amounts of grains and produce for shipping to the big city. But, with the "roads" in such unreliable and deplorable condition, transportation presented a major problem.

Not only were the roads treacherous, the wagons and carts were just as unreliable, fragile and prone to breaking down. At about this time, German and English craftsmen designed a new wagon, based on the same concepts used in their homelands, and developed a sturdy, rugged, large capacity, heavyweight vehicle. It became known as the Conestoga Wagon.

The behemoth sized Conestoga stood about 26 feet in length and 11 feet high; it served as the tractor-trailer truck of its day. The wagon's narrow width and large wheels enabled it to maneuver the deeply rutted and narrow roads, and even mud rarely stopped it for long. An empty wagon weighed almost two tons, and the cost to build ran approximately $250. Constructed almost entirely with hand tools, the wagon revolutionized the transportation of goods and people over the rugged hills and valleys of Pennsylvania. The wagon received its name from the place it originated, the Conestoga Valley of Lancaster County. By 1750, there were approximately 7,000 Conestoga wagons on the roads of Pennsylvania.

Back to the letter...back to "I'll be there with bells on."

The roads were busy and timely passage critical. Delays were costly, and it did not take much for the narrow, unpaved roads to backup, creating traffic jams, just like today. Very few among the traders enjoyed the reputation that "old Jake" did. He almost always delivered his goods on time, a sign of superior driving ability, or of incredible luck – a source of real pride to the wagon-master.

Almost every wagon had a set of bells mounted somewhere. As the wagon entered town, the bells rang

"Do not turn the wheels of a wagon... backwards while greasing... or they will have a breakdown, or cause witches to bother you."
- Superstitions of the Pennsylvania Germans

gaily, announcing the arrival of that particular trader. A typical wagon had four to six horses, and between each pair of horses hung bells of various sizes made of brass or iron. Needless to say, they created quite a tune while riding along! The bells were a trader's pride and joy, a proud and independent group that considered it an embarrassment to be without their bells.

And "old Jake" had the best of bells, and he took great care of them. He became a legend in Strasburg, warmly welcomed by the town folk, always arriving on time with badly needed supplies. Jake's route usually took him to Philadelphia, a long journey when traveling only 12 to 14 miles a day over the most treacherous of roads. Dependable and tough, Jake always arrived with his bells ringing, for which town folk adored him.

Missing bells usually meant only one thing. Somewhere on your journey you encountered trouble. Perhaps your wagon became stuck, or it broke down and needed repair. Either way, you needed help. The help could come in many forms, from any of the varied travelers along the way. However, a code existed between the traders who shared the roadways. In lieu of payment in silver or goods, a fellow trader could demand payment in the form of your bells. Whether to embarrass your fellow trader or to gain a competitive advantage, everyone knew what missing bells meant.

Thus, the day "old Jake" appeared in Strasburg without his bells, everyone instantly knew that he had lost his bells to a fellow trader. Jake went about making his deliveries but would not answer any questions about the missing bells. Obviously upset, he exited at the west end of town, and no one ever saw Jake again.

Some time later, Jake's coveted Conestoga wagon

Strasburg auction grounds.

turned up at the Franklin Street auction. Many swore they could hear Jake's distinctive bells ringing throughout the entire auction. His wagon sold and disappeared from town for the last time.

But the same cannot be said of those bells. People continued to hear bells ringing at the auction decades after "old Jake" disappeared. And many

claim that to this day you can hear bells ring as you enter the public cemetery just across

> phantom traveler: ...doomed to eternal wandering as punishment for some folly or sin...
>   - Ancient Folklore

the way from the Franklin Street auction site.

Perhaps "old Jake" has returned to Strasburg... with bells on!

Ghost Tour Update:

Guests on the ghost tour have admitted to hearing bells while on Franklin Street in the vicinity of the Strasburg auction ground. This is reported *before* hearing the tale of "Old Jake." Some also claim to hear the bells near the gates of the cemetery.

Several tour guides have mentioned a problem with their lantern while telling this story near the little cemetery beside the auction grounds. For no discernible reason, the stable, flat bottom lanterns occasionally fall over – scaring not only the guests, but the tour guide as well. Maybe "old Jake" is just making his presence known.

John Funck House

The method for finding ghost stories assumes many forms, persistence being the most important. Unlike "ghost-hunters," who perform investigations searching for orbs, ectoplasm and spirals of energy using scientific equipment such as digital cameras, heat sensing devices and electromagnetic meters, ghost-story-hunting requires old-fashioned legwork, word of mouth clues and historic research.

The hunt for the ghost of the John Funck house started as most do...with the question, "Did you know this place is haunted?"

A 1997 visit to the dress shop located on East Main Street in Strasburg just a few doors from the center square led to the story of a mysterious haunting of one of the oldest buildings in town. No longer a dress shop, today, a gift shop and a flower shop reside under the old tin-roof, and like many structures near the center of small Pennsylvania towns, it bears a varied and sometimes unknown history.

John Funck built the structure in 1798 and lived there with his wife. In its more than two hundred year history it served in various capacities. Among them a colonial tavern, a second floor artist studio and until 1966, as the Strasburg post office. The late 1800s saw a Victorian storefront added, and sometime along the

> John Funck: Strasburg's "renaissance man" and a local land baron. Also an accomplished painter, successful millwright and innkeeper. Instrumental in forming the Strasburg Scientific Society. Funck built a "flying machine" which he launched from the roof of his house, crashing onto the street below. He survived the experiment.

way, renovations resulted in two shops, as it stands today.

Initially, the only information on ghostly activity came from the store clerk, who mentioned that she heard footsteps upstairs, even though no one else occupied the building (the shop next door had not opened yet).

A short time later, while visiting the new gift shop, the off-hand inquiry on whether they were bothered by the ghosts upstairs brought a frown and worried response, "All the time."

They, too, heard footsteps upstairs, but they had other unexplainable incidents to report. The front door would open by itself, and most of the employees avoided venturing into the basement, unless absolutely necessary, because of the narrow dark stairs and the feeling of dread when down there. The basement also scared off an electrician, who, after spending hours working alone in the basement, left abruptly before completing the job and would not come back.

Unexplained manifestations seem to have affected one employee in particular. His ordinary leg brace only gives off static electricity while in the shop, and he witnessed the apparition of a young woman standing in the doorway. He described her as a misty form, in a plain, long dress and wearing an old-fashioned cap. When told that a tavern once occupied the building

periwinkle: ...Hang over doorways...to keep out witches and spirits...
- French folklore

he exclaimed, "That's what she looked like - a tavern girl!"

A self-proclaimed psychic from New York, who stopped in to shop, described a similar image of a girl at the front door as she entered the shop. She went on to say that she felt two spirits occupied the building.

When the flower shop opened next door in 1999, the new tenants experienced "some trouble," as they describe it. Initially, they blamed long hours and overactive imaginations, but so many weird coincidences happened, they felt the only explanation could be the supernatural. Plagued by lights, faucets and appliances going on and off on their own and an uneasy feeling, as if someone unseen were present, typified their experiences.

One night, following a 15-hour shift, the front door would not lock despite repeated attempts. The key just would not turn the lock. Exasperated and befuddled, the exhausted shopkeeper finally blurted out, "I promise I'll be back." As strange as it sounds, the key turned and the door locked.

However, the second floor seems to evoke the *most* uncomfortable feelings of all. One particular spot at the top of the steps where a small landing exists, brought a puzzled statement from one of the clerks, "I get the strangest feeling right here. I don't know why." Continuing down the hall, and with an apprehensive look on her face she said, "Many

What's going on upstairs?

times when I come up here, the faucet is on. I'm the only one here, there's no one else who could possibly get up here."

So here we have it... incidents that occur on regular basis in this historic 18th century building. Why? Who could be haunting the old building with such a varied history?

The library turned up some interesting tidbits, but nothing definitive. Finally, a few inquiries around town turned up an old-timer who remembered when the post office still operated in that building. He also recalled that a man shot himself upstairs! Sometimes, persistence is enough to make the hair on the back of your neck stand up!

GHOST STORIES OF LANCASTER, PA

Acknowledgements

Editor: Alanna Lynne Reeser

Acorn Press, Inc. *Inside the Fulton Opera House.*
Adams III, Charles J. *Pennsylvania Dutch Country Ghosts Legends and Lore*
Aurand, Jr., A. Monroe. *Popular Home Remedies and Superstitions of the Pennsylvania Germans*
Boker, George. "The Legend of the Hounds"
Dieffenbach, Susan. *Cornwall Iron Furnace*
Fiedel, Dorothy B. *Official Ghost Guide to Lancaster County Pennsylvania*
Graduating Class of Strasburg High School 1926. *History of Strasburg*
Guiley, RoseMary Ellen. *The Encyclopedia of Ghosts and Spirits*
Historic Preservation Trust of Lancaster 1985, The. *"Our Present Past" an Update of Lancaster's Heritage*
Historical Papers and Addresses of the Lancaster County Historical Society. Vol. XXV. *The Strasburg Scientific Society*
Kelley, Jr., Joseph J. *Life and Times in Colonial Philadelphia*
Lestz, George S. *Historic Heart of Lancaster*
Miller, E. Willard. *Pennsylvania, Keystone to Progress, An Illustrated History*
Noble, Richard E. *The Touch of Time*
Reninger, Marion Wallace. *Orange Street*
Spotts, Charles D. *They Called It Strasburg*
Strasburg Heritage Society 1994. *A Strolling Tour of Strasburg's Historic District.*
Van Doren, Carl. *Benjamin Franklin*
Wood, Jr., Jerome H. *Conestoga Crossroads, Lancaster, Pennsylvania 1730-1790*

John F. Reynolds images: Courtesy of Archives and Special Collections, Franklin and Marshall College, Lancaster, PA

Fulton Opera House
Historic Preservation Trust of Lancaster County
Historic Strasburg Inn

Intelligencer Journal, New Era, Sunday News. Lancaster, PA.
Lancaster County Historical Society
Strasburg Weekly News. Strasburg, PA
www.afrolumens.org
www.nga.gov

Patricia Fackler
Barry Kornhauser
Shirley and Al Seeley
Eileen Reeser, who collected much of the material for the Strasburg stories.
All former and current guides from the Ghosts of Lancaster, PA walking tour.